NATHAN PETERSON

Dance Again

Grief is Healing

For my family, for our friends, and for Olivia.

What About
These Moments?

On March 11, 2016, we said goodbye to our daughter. She was not supposed to live at all - she was deemed "incompatible with life" before she was born - but Olivia lived for 14 months.

14 impossible, beautiful months. All of the pain and uncertainty of those months was worth it. We would do it again. Every moment.

But what about *these* moments?

These moments of depression. Hopelessness. Darkness.

These moments of marital distance. Blame. Hate.

These moments of isolation. Loneliness. Embarrassment.

These moments of loss of all certainty about life, death,

God, hopes and dreams, health, finances, everything.

What about these moments? Are *these* moments beautiful?

After Olivia passed away, I published my previous book, "So Am I", to share what we had learned during her life. I had been writing it since she was born. It's about truly living, *resting*, in the midst of uncertainty and fear. It's about our battle as human beings, to *be*, to choose to live each moment.

Immediately after publishing "So Am I", I fell into darkness. I wanted to celebrate my accomplishment, but deep down I felt I had just packaged up everything left in me and shipped it away. I had nothing left. Olivia was gone. I had nothing more to offer.

Which leads to this book, another 14 months later, this idea: "Dance Again".

The previous book was my chance to articulate what I learned during Olivia's life. This is my chance to practice it.

"Dance Again" is my practice. It is my process: of grieving, of hurting, of healing, of depression, of anger, of hope, of *being*. It is my life, my journey, during the 14 months following Olivia's burial.

The following pages contain, once again, everything left in me. Much of it is not pleasant; all of it is real. I hope the life and beauty, the heartache and rage, resonate with something inside you. Perhaps it will even stir a part of you which has been waiting to be awakened.

Thank you for traveling these 14 months with me.

March 11, 2016 (the morning before Olivia passed away)

Another long night with Livie. I got maybe 4hrs of sleep. Heather got maybe 2. Olivia didn't ever sleep. I feel fat, tired, confused, overwhelmed, disinterested. I probably have a very limited amount to give today. I want to give it to my family.

Heather and I fought this morning so we don't really have each other at the moment.

It's sunny out. That's nice.

I had a nice breakfast and coffee.

So tired, my brain is fuzzy.

Have patience with yourself. Do what you can but don't imagine a deadline. Things can take a month instead of a day. There is a difference between hiding and allowing things to develop.

Enjoy the process.

OLIVIA'S FUNERAL NOTES

TODAY X photo - JPG (call R + let him know)

SUN
~~SUN~~
~~SUN~~
~~SAT~~
~~SUN~~

X Marty meeting
X send new pic to Randy
X post update on ~~funeral~~ service on Facebook
X donation link (send to Randy)
X schedule w Marty
X plan concept for service w H
~~gather any needed media for service~~
X get clothes for services

MON
- kids can pick something for casket
X drop blanket & leggings (by noon)
~~cemetery meeting~~

X @ 11 Marriage
@ cemetery

~~purchase guest register~~
~~plan service~~
@ 1:30 Marty meeting

X call Marilyn

- prep sharing
- prep songs
X send media h M.
(video, JPG, mp3, txt)

UES
@ 10-11 private time
@ 11:30 funeral / visitation

WED @ 10 private burial

March 19, 2016

This was a long week, to say the least. Long. Hard. Beautiful. Horrible. Perfect.

Now it's over. Olivia is gone. How?? I miss her so much.

I also feel relieved. I feel guilty about that. I feel emptiness. Our family feels so different. I don't know how I feel.

I keep wanting to ask the question, "what's next?" It feels too early to ask but impossible to ignore. There's just no answer. What's next?? How would I even know?

I don't want to go to the next thing. I also don't want to sit here. So many conflicting feelings. So much turmoil.

I'm so cloudy.

I miss Olivia. I'm afraid of not missing her.

I'm so… foggy.

I Don't Feel Like Writing

I don't feel like writing. I don't feel like singing. I don't feel like practicing. Or being a parent, or getting dressed. I don't feel like much of anything. Is this depression? Probably.

This isn't a cry for help or even a complaint. I expected to feel like this. Storms come. The battle can't be about stopping the storm or even feeling better about the storm.

My battle is to *allow it to be what it is*.

Today, my battle was to let myself feel bad. Also to finish a song. To clean the toys out of the yard. To play with my kids and read Frozen to my daughter before bed. It wasn't easy. It didn't feel good.

Eventually, good feelings will come. The clouds will part. Blue sky will emerge. I will laugh. Things will be fine. But until then, I choose to be okay with what is.

I choose to be okay with feeling bad. And missing Olivia. And feeling broken and incomplete. I choose to allow it to be what it is.

The sight of dead grass, brown lifeless trees, and overcast skies is overwhelming. But under the surface, life is coming. Spring is coming.

Maybe life is still ahead…

I still can't believe she's gone.
The worst part is, her whole life
feels like a dream...
Like it never happened.

The most beautiful thing
Just stopped
With it, my heart did t
Everything else keeps mov
breathing, growing
laughing, shining.
I've (We're) just... stopped
with you.

supposed to keep livin - to move on

March 27, 2016

Heather and I just had the biggest fight.

It seems obvious that today would be a monumental battle between us. We played together on stage for the first time in 17 months, since before Livie was born. We're new people now. Us cooperating musically and publicly is… important. Powerful. Meaningful. Restorative. Of course it wasn't easy.

Still, what happened tonight?

March 31, 2016

This week I released a new single. For the rest of this month, what's important? I need to catch up on exercise. I want to get back to voice practice. I need to keep moving forward with my writing and recording.

What about being sad? What about Olivia? Am I over that? Have I just moved on? I'm not crying much about it now. Is that bad? I feel scared that I'm going to not miss her… or I'll forget her… or I'll just go back to who I was and it'll be like a dream - like it never happened.

April 10, 2016

I'm feeling more and more lost, in a fog. I guess it has to do with Olivia, but I'm not thinking about her directly. I'm just feeling bad. I've just lost the will to… care. It's just hard to care.

The only thing that makes me feel better is buying new gadgets… or trying new coffee recipes… or eating. It's all consumption.

Oh. *I'm empty.*

April 11, 2016

We visited Olivia's grave today. I think we're still in shock. It's still hard to believe she's gone.

We're trying to let it all (the feelings, the conflicting emotions, the frustration, confusion, all of it) just be what it is when it is. We're trying to practice the living of life-in-the-here-and-now the way we learned to do while Olivia was alive. It's harder now.

Where You Are

One month ago we woke up from a full eight hours of sleep, for the first time in 14 months. The sun was up, the birds were singing. Our boys were playing video games and Ruth was watching Frozen and eating her third frozen waffle. I felt physical energy - that was new. But for the first time in 14 months, we woke up to a world without Olivia. "Where is our daughter?!"

For the past month, Heather and I have woken up to this new reality. We have slept and have felt physical renewal. We have received renewal from countless friends who have sent notes, cards, food, love, and prayers. We are still being carried, but we feel more worn down now than we did when we slept only two to four hours a night. There is really no differentiating between body and spirit - it is all a part of me. And I am worn down. I am thankful for the sleep, definitely. But while we were not getting sleep before, our hearts were *filled* with the love and joy which flowed from Olivia. Our love sustained her. Her love sustained us too.

We found a way to live when Olivia was here. It felt impossible, but it was either (a) crawl into a ball and let worry and fear paralyze us or (b) return our attention to *now*, and do only the next thing.

That's all any of us can do. That's what Heather and I will learn to do again, eventually.

If I was to give advice to my Month-1-of-Olivia's-Life-Self, it would be this:

Come back to where you are. In this moment, everything is good. Even if it's hard, it's real, and it's good. Your baby is alive and you are holding her. Do that. The future will come later. Do not get there before it comes. You will be okay if you stay. Be where you are. This is living.

This is good advice for today too.

Still Alive

I think we have moved beyond the heavy non-stop crying phase of grieving, at least for now. This new phase makes me miss the heavy crying. I'm not sure how to describe it. "Nothing", maybe, or a dull ache.

Every time I see a photo of Livie I'm suddenly pulled back to the reality that she existed. I forget. How am I already forgetting she was here? It feels like a dream. Did it even happen? Was she really here? Where is she now? She isn't in the past. The photos aren't her. She isn't in the ground. I want to dig her up and hold her body again, but it would not be her. Every time I see a photo of her, I touch it. It doesn't work. It isn't her. Her being in heaven isn't working for me either. The truth does not work.

Nothing "works".

She isn't here.

And a bigger problem is, neither am I. I'm somewhere

else, maybe trying to find her so I can bring her back into the safety of our family. I don't know. Our other three kids finally have us back, but we are still not back. It isn't fair to them, which is frustrating.

And where is God? It was obvious He was with us when she was here. We were living in the middle of a miracle. Now we're just… floating around. There is no direction; just floating around, sort-of here, mostly absent, still terrified. "What's next? If I couldn't protect Olivia, how will I protect the rest of my family?"

This is what I need to hear today:

What is seemingly dead is still alive.

While your heart aches and your mind panics and tries to find Olivia, while you lay in pain and teeter on insanity, you are being restored. So is your family. So is Olivia.

I know it feels like chaos, but there is a plan, a process. This moment is a part of the process. The pain is a part of the process. The insanity is a part of the process. Do not fight it. Let it.

Olivia is not lost. Neither are you. The Current has you both. Trust the Current. Trust the process.

These Two Years

Today I feel good. I also feel bad. I feel energy. I also feel lethargic. I miss Olivia. I am also happy her suffering is over. I miss Olivia, but I am also glad to finally sleep again. I feel hope for the future. I am also drowning in the pain and exhaustion of the past two years.

I can't make any sense of these conflicting emotions.

We just went through the most difficult thing we have ever experienced. I carried my daughter's body. I placed her in a basket. Some person I had never met took her out my front door.

After Olivia's burial service we were supposed to drive away so they could take care of the logistics of removing the chairs and burying her. As we drove away my fatherly instinct told me not to leave until she was safe. I parked the car a couple hundred feet away, and through some trees, we watched as two men picked her up and put her in the hole. A tractor covered her with dirt. They loaded up their truck and drove away. It was quiet. It was finished. I turned the van around and drove back to the site. Heather and I got out and stood at Olivia's grave. That was it. We had just completed the most difficult and horrible thing either of us ever imagined enduring. So had Olivia. And *it was good*. Beautiful. The most wonderful and rich and life-giving thing I have ever experienced.

These were the hardest two years of my life. Also, they were the best. All of my future years will be better because of these ones. If there was a button I could push to remove the pain or change what happened, I would smash it to pieces without hesitation.

I can't make any sense of these conflicting emotions. But I do know, all of them are real. I choose to feel them, to let them exist without trying to reconcile them or understand them.

I am tired and worn and weak. Also, I am filled with strength. My heart is torn to shreds. Also, it is well with my soul.

My heart is torn
to shreds.
Also, it is well
with my soul.

Grow

I was worried about this flower. But apparently, it didn't know it was supposed to die.

The only thing harder than missing Olivia has been seeing Heather miss her. No mother should be separated from her baby. No mother should have to feel a permanent attachment, this invisible cord, connecting her to a grave a mile away. They both sleep in the middle of the night, connected. That time that used to be Olivia's and ours is now just an ache, an emptiness, and we have this illogical urge to go get Olivia's body. We know she isn't in the grave. Maybe she is even closer; I really don't know. But her little body is there, and aside from the toys and clothes and burp cloths still laying around the house, that little body is the only thing we have left.

My wife's heart is broken. The beautiful thing is that I know she would do it again in a heartbeat. Heather chose a broken heart. That is the best example of love I have ever seen.

Olivia is like this flower. She did not know the protocol for living life. She just grew however she did until the end.

I think we will be like this flower too. I no longer care to grow in a straight, typical line. Even if I did, what control do I really have? I can't stop my child from dying; I can't protect her. I can't stop my wife's heart from breaking.

This is just life - broken hearts, funerals, lightsaber fights, never-ending Frozen music, and all.

Today, I will breathe in. I will breathe out. I will allow for the pain and anger and confusion and discrepancies. I will trust that we will continue to grow, whatever that looks like.

We're still here. We're breathing out, we're breathing in, we're alive. And maybe life is still ahead...

Fear at the Door, Rest Inside

In the spring of 2012, I heard this word, **"Rest."** I realized how horrible I was at it. I wasn't even sure what it was. Was it extra sleep? Was it not working on Sundays? Shortly after I heard this word, my life began changing. For one reason or another, one by one, the things with which I occupied myself were stripped away until I found myself with nothing left to hold.

A year later I was in a panic, wondering how we were going to make ends meet. Everything in me said to do what I had always done: get on email, get on the phone, make the next thing happen. Anyone who knew me knew I was someone who could make anything happen. If I didn't know how, I bought a book and learned. Anything I ever wanted I found a way to get.

Then I heard the word again, **"Rest."**

"What?! Now? No. My family is depending on me. My reputation is at stake. I don't have time for rest. I will rest when things are okay."

"No. That is not what rest is."

Rest is not something you do. Rest is something you put on. It is something you *are* while you do what you are doing. Rest is a posture.

I decided to do the exact opposite thing my insides were telling me to do. I went to the backyard, sat on a chair, and watched. I did not know what I was watching for. I listened. I did not know what I was listening for. Every time a thought or an idea came to my head, I wrote it down and then resumed sitting. It was horrible, like ignoring an itch for hours. I knew that if it was this hard for me to physically sit still, it was important for me to learn. If my body could not sit still, then how could my mind or my heart? So I decided to discipline myself to sit that way at least one day a week.

Eventually, I sat this way more often. Meanwhile, my professional life continued to fall apart and the temptation to do something about it grew. I heard so many voices, some from friends and family but most from my own head:

"You're lazy."

"You're being irresponsible."

"What are you doing??!!"

"It's up to you to provide for your family."

"Get up and make something happen, now!"

Simultaneously I heard another voice:

"Rest."

"How long do I wait?"

"Rest."

This was the summer of 2013. A year later, we received the call about our soon-to-be-born baby's condition. I had thought that the urge to get up and do something was strong before, but now this was on an entirely new level. Again I heard the voice say "Rest", so we didn't research Trisomy 18. We didn't look for different doctors who would say something we wanted to hear.

I continued to sit and stare at the fence, quieting my body, and eventually, at times, quieting my mind and my heart as well. I can not even describe the amount of Fear that was present. But this time it was different. It was as if in the past Fear had walked in the door and I was afraid; now Fear stood in the doorway and waited to be invited in. More and more Fear gathered at the door, but it did not come in. It only waited. I could see it there. It was terrifying. But I wasn't able to invite it in. Rest was occupying the space instead.

The moments in the hospital on January 7th 2015 - I thought my wife might die. I expected to hold our lifeless baby that morning. I knew I would speak at Olivia's funeral and not know what to say. It was like a nightmare. But I remember it. I was there. If she would have lived only an hour, I would have been there for that one hour. Because Fear was at the door, but Rest was inside. My posture was rest, quiet, and trust. It was not about making things happen. It was about watching, listening, and being there and nowhere else. I was not going to miss it, as horrible as it could have been.

During the first few months of Olivia's life, Fear kept congregating at the door. We thought we saw her last breath so many times. We were so sleep deprived. I passed out one day just walking across the room. At this point, I felt pretty incapable of getting up and making something happen. The doctors were clear that there was nothing we could do. Hospice was at our house every few days. I was not tempted to get up and do something about Olivia. Now I was tempted to get up and work. To make sure the bills got paid. To make sure my career did not disappear any more than it already had. But underneath was a stronger need: to run, to get the hell out of this situation. Work can be an easy place for a man to avoid the realities of his life. It was pretty obvious though, that work was not to be my focus - that whatever time we had left with Olivia was to be cherished - every minute of it. Still, I felt the urge to run more than ever.

"Rest."

I continued to hold the posture. To sit. To stare at the fence. To listen quietly. I was not going to miss it.

I was there the whole time. All 14 months of her life.

I lost my posture at times. But I can say that the 30-year-old Nathan (five years ago) would have occupied himself the entire time, trying to make things happen, running like crazy away from the pain. No. I had practiced for this all year. I knew how to allow the itch, the pain, to be there and not to move. I knew how to allow the voices in my head and the voices from others to be there without being influenced by them. I knew how to go deeper within my Self, to the place where a still and quiet voice whispered the word "Rest" over and over. I had practiced the posture; the time had come to use it. I was there the whole time. I did not miss my daughter's life.

In March of 2016, when I got the call that Olivia had stopped breathing, I was on a bike ride with our other three kids. Time stopped. Jude asked if Olivia was okay, and I was able to look at him and say, "Yes. Even if she does die, all of us are okay."

We rode our bikes so fast. Fear was now filling the doorway and had crowded around the house and the windows and as far as the eye could see. We rode our bikes. I didn't feel much, but the tears streaming down my face told me, "Today is the day. It is finished." We kept riding.

I don't remember getting off my bike. I'm guessing I had never run so fast. But I will never forget the feeling of walking through the back porch door and seeing Heather and Olivia there. The most sinking and unreal amount of pain I have ever felt mixed with an equal amount of peace, beauty, and a sense of victory.

After a lot of crying, the only words I could say to Heather were, "We did it." We won. Olivia won. Heather won. I won. Our family won. Our community won. Yes, Olivia died, but that was never the battle we were fighting. We had chosen to fight Fear instead.

I don't think I have experienced the remainder of that day, or the next few days, or the funeral or the burial yet. I think I'm still back processing the day Olivia was born. It's weird. I have never grieved like this before, but I think the body has a way of pacing how much pain it allows in at once. I'm realizing now that we will be experiencing the pain and the beauty of Olivia's life and death for a long time. I don't know if or when we will ever feel normal or even functional again. But I do remember one thing about the morning after Olivia died, vividly.

I remember going for a run and the feeling of Rest overwhelming me. Not happiness or excitement - I was very sad - but so much Rest. And I remember noticing how little Fear I sensed, like it was not even at the door anymore. It was as if the battle had ended and Fear had lost and it just turned and went home. There was no temptation to

34

run or to make anything happen. Olivia was dead but I felt an amazing amount of Rest. And trust. And quiet. And strength.

Since that day, Fear has returned to my door. I have struggled more than ever to rest. This battle is never-ending. But once you win one battle, every battle after is different. Now you know you can win. You know what it feels like to say "we did it" and you know you can do it again.

I have a feeling the next year is going to be more difficult to rest than the previous two years were. That is a very overwhelming thought. But I have a wife and three living kids and one sleeping daughter who need a husband and a father who knows how to rest. That is what I will choose to do.

Fear at the door, Rest inside.

May 24, 2016

Today I feel heartbroken.

This week has been one of the hardest ones. I have no idea why, which could be why it is so hard.

It is 70 degrees and sunny. The kids are at school. Heather is out. My guitar and notebook are here. But I don't want to write a song. I don't have a song in me… or I have a thousand but none are accessible.

I should go outside and take a walk, but I don't want to do that either. I want to want to…

I feel permanently broken. Not the person in the movie who at some point wipes away their final tear, gets up and does something wonderful. I am the one who no one made a movie about because there is nothing marketable about a guy whose heart breaks and stays broken.

Brokenhearted and non-movie-worthy. That is the status today.

Brokenhearted
AND
Non-Movie-Worthy

This Path

I have run this path so many times.

The path has never changed, but I have.

I ran this path as a 22-year-old who wanted to be a great pastor. I thought I was invincible and wise. Deeper down, I felt like a nobody.

I ran this path while my marriage was in shambles. I didn't know (Heather has since filled me in) - I couldn't have known - I was too preoccupied making my mark.

I ran this path at 28, knowing I had "made it". I was playing for thousands and I was sure things were about to break wide open.

I ran this path as a leader.

As a mentor.

As an authority.

As a winner.

Deeper down, I still felt like a nobody.

I ran this path as a new father who was learning the value of sleep.

I ran this path at 32, praying to God, "Let the Current take me wherever it wants. Help me to let go."

I ran this path realizing I had failed my wife.

I ran this path realizing I had failed my kids, already.

I ran this path realizing how much I was driven by fear, and how much I was afraid of quietness and Rest.

I ran this path in major turmoil at work, in exhaustion with my band, and in disconnection from my family.

I ran this path realizing I did not want to be a worship pastor anymore.

I ran this path realizing I did not want to lead worship at conferences anymore.

I ran this path longing for quiet.

For trust.

For Rest.

I ran this path at 33, no longer a worship pastor. No longer a worship leader. No longer able to make sound with my voice. I let go of my plans on this road.

On this road lie my plans.

I ran in silence.

I ran in quiet.

I ran this path at 34, listening to a book about worry.

I ran a little slower. I was tired of running.

I ran this path, listing my worries, mouthing the words, "I choose to trust: to trust God, to trust myself, to trust the process", and literally throwing my hands behind me, symbolizing my leaving the worries behind me, on this road.

On this road lie my worries.

I ran this path knowing I was going to experience the death of my daughter.

I ran this path wondering what I would say at her funeral.

I ran this path knowing I was afraid to name her.

Olivia.

I ran this path as Olivia's father.

I ran this path realizing we were now the parents of a severely disabled child, maybe forever.

I ran this path at 35, realizing my life was now this little girl, our immediate family, and nothing else.

On this road lie my dreams.

I ran this path crying to God for relief, for help, for hope, for a single night of sleep.

I ran this path the morning after Olivia died. The air was crisp. The path seemed inviting. The running felt different. Less about running from something, or to something. It was just running.

I ran this path missing Olivia, unable to see through the tears; having to stop, breathe, write down my thoughts, and start again.

Today I run this path again. I run past my plans and my worries. I run past my dreams. I run past my tears. I run in the footsteps of a thousand other Me's. But none of them are me.

It is the same road. It is a one-mile stretch in a dumpy neighborhood. It seems like there is no way this path could ever take you anywhere. But it does take you there.

It is not about the path. It is about what happens in you *as you travel* that brings you to where you are going. The externals are only a path for you to use while you do the real work inside. You are becoming who you are. *That* is where you are going.

The path has never changed, but I have.

Today I run this path confused.

Heartbroken.

Determined.

Exhausted.

Empty.

But alive.

"Success"

Last night I dreamt about Olivia all night. I dreamt Heather dug her up and was holding her. She looked fine. No decay. She was moving. I have this dream often. I always think, "Wait, are we sure she's dead? She's moving!" Everyone in the dream tells me it is totally normal and that she is dead. But last night she talked. She said she loved me, Jude, Charlie, Ruth, and Heather. "*Are we sure she's dead?!* She just spoke, for crying out loud." "Yes, that's normal." They put her in a big cold room to freeze her, for some reason. There were other children there too. One by one the children began waking up. They were fine. After all the kids were alive, Olivia started breathing. Over the following days, she started eating. She was growing. She was alive.

I woke up feeling like I never slept. I spent the entire evening with Olivia, again, like the old days, watching her do things everyone said were impossible for her to do and being amazed by her determination, strength, and beauty. I watched as her fighting brought so many others to life. That is what she did.

Today I made breakfast for the family, helped clean up, did yoga and pull-ups, and did voice practice. I went outside for a run and there were four baby birds on the sidewalk. Two were still breathing. I lost it. I picked them up and put them on the grass, together, so they were touching. I don't know; maybe that will bring the two living ones some comfort for their last moments. I am obviously hyper-sensitive right now. I wish I could take care of those birds. I didn't touch them with my skin but I wanted to. I wish I could touch Olivia again.

I saw a 14-year-old girl with Downs at the pool this weekend. She came right up to me and stared in my face. I don't know why she did, but all I could think was, "We were ready for that. We were ready for the wheelchairs and the care-taking. We were ready to give up our lives." Now we "have our lives back," but we don't want it. We want Olivia.

There are more important things than "doing well", than "success." We found one of them. Heather and I do not want "success" anymore. We want life.

This Moment

I don't think there is anything more difficult than noticing what is in front of you - than being where you are, when you are.

Three years ago I wanted to be in a different city.

Last year I wanted to feel "normal" again.

This year I want to be in last year, with Olivia.

But here I am. Here. Today.

What is happening in this moment?

My son is practicing piano upstairs.

My daughter is playing with her dolls.

My other son is stomping around the house because he is bored and wants to make us all pay.

My wife is up there trying to create some sense of order.

Olivia is at rest a mile away… or a million miles away, I don't know.

I'm tired from another restless night, with dreams of my family being in danger and my inability to keep them safe.

I'm sitting in my office trying to put my feelings into words.

The grass is wet from a storm which just ended. The sun is peeking out from behind the clouds.

This is life at the moment. And at the moment, everything is okay. And even if it was not, this is life.

How many of our years will we give away to Fear? How much of our own life will we not live?

Don't be gone. Don't let this happen over and over, to us and our kids and their kids. If we lose the battle, they will too. Let's break the cycle, of dying before we are dead. Let's return to where we are, when we are, and who we are. Let's leave what is not, alone. Those times and places will come, or they won't. If we can learn to be here now, we will have the discipline to be there then.

No matter how painful or confusing or perfect, Life is only here. It is only now.

June 11, 2016

How did I feel this week? Pretty bad.

Lots of sickness in the family.

I felt tired.

I couldn't sleep.

I felt crabby.

Unmotivated.

Not fun to be around.

I feel like I'm just floundering. I can't make anything happen so I'm just practicing a lot… and waiting. It's really hard. Boring. Scary.

Someone shot a gun a few blocks from our house yesterday. What am I doing to keep my family safe?! Shouldn't I be making sure we have money and getting us moved? My business is in debt over its head.

Have I failed? Should I do something else?

Now, think about this week with a different mindset.

Okay.

What did I do?

I played a concert for a couple who lost their daughter. I helped them grieve.

I practiced every day. I made progress.

I exercised daily. Yoga and running.

I made breakfast daily for my family.

I took the kids Friday to the pool all day when Heather was sick.

H and I had a counseling session.

I started a new song.

I made a blog post.

I fixed the light in the bathroom.

I mowed the lawn.

I finished reading a book.

I put the kids to bed every night.

I read to Ruth every night.

I went to baseball with the boys three times this week.

I did all of this while feeling sick.

I did it all while grieving Olivia.

Today is three months since she died.

I choose not to fill the emptiness.
I choose not to try to appear "productive".
I choose not to rush out of this.
I choose to rest and to trust.

I choose quiet.

I choose to live, here.

June 27, 2016

I feel blank inside.

I know there is a ton of pain in there somewhere, and I am (1) afraid to touch it because it has been covered up for a few days and I am getting used to feeling numb, and (2) feeling very guilty for not doing my "grief work" like a good little griever.

I feel on display, as if everyone is watching to see how I handle things. I have always felt like that. I feel the world on my shoulders.

I feel angry, like, "Really? We had to go through all of this, Livie had to go through all of it, so we could be made into an example? And what now? What are we now? Olivia is gone and we are still here. We are used up. Tossed aside. No longer useful or interesting. We don't have the energy we used to have. We don't have the creativity we used to feel, or the patience, or the motivation.

Another part of me would not change a single thing about any of it. Screw our example. Screw what happens next. Those 14 months with Olivia (and even these past few months in its wake, here with Heather and our other three kids), they are the most treasured months of my life.

I feel equal parts of "what now?" and "who cares, I can't take another step anyway."

I know tomorrow will be different. Probably later today will be different. And I hesitate to write this without tying some sort of bow around it, partially because I would like to write something inspiring but mostly because I do not want people to try to fix it.

There is nothing to be fixed; it is what it is. And even if it could be fixed, we would not want it. Our pain is what connects us to Olivia. Our pain is what progresses us through the grieving process.

Yesterday, our friend Mike told me apologetically that he was standing at Olivia's grave and did not know what to pray for us. He wanted to help, but all he could do was stand there and feel sad. I felt so thankful for his willingness to sit in our pain with us, rather than looking for a way out. This is the most helpful and loving thing a friend can do. Thank you, Mike.

July 12, 2016

Yesterday was four months since Olivia died.

Heather and I feel like we have disappeared from the earth. We obviously had to live in a different reality while she was here. Since she has been gone it has felt like we are neither here nor there; we are not with Olivia anymore, but we can not go back to our way of life before her either. So we are just sort-of nowhere. Or, it feels that way. But I think this "nowhere" is actually somewhere… maybe even somewhere infinitely important.

The Courage To Be

A community of people. Human beings. Not fixing each other. Not controlling each other. But laughing together. Crying together. Hurting together. Feeling together. Being together.

It takes so much courage. Way more courage than it takes to act. Or accomplish. Or acquire. The courage to *be*. It requires quiet, rest, trust - a total shift of our mindset.

It is a coming back to where we are. To the present. To ourselves. To each other. Anywhere else is alone. We are here. Now. This is where all of the beauty and love and community exists. It is also where all of the pain and heartache and failure and where Fear is. This is where Life is.

Be. Any other activity is meaningless. Our most powerful and meaningful expression of humanity is right in front of us. It has never been more available than it is, right now.

Pushing Heaven Off

I was at church. I had to leave. I could not listen for another minute to someone telling about how great God is and about how everything we see and feel and know right now is inconsequential.

I'm tired of the theoretical ethereal telling about life. I need something real, now. I need to feel the ground under my feet. I need to breathe air.

I need to *experience* God, not just know *about* God.

I don't believe there is such a huge divide between this life and the next - that nothing here and now carries over. Something will carry over.

I don't believe Olivia will be perfect in heaven, at least not "perfect" the way we mean it. In heaven, Olivia's ears may still be lower than normal. Both her eyes may still not track together. Her hair may be the same untamable super-villain hair it was when she was here. At least, I hope so. I love those things about her.

Is heaven really a place where everyone is "perfect", or could it be that our definition of "perfect" changes in heaven? Could it be that our mindset shifts, and not the circumstance?

No one knows what God and heaven are like. I wish we would stop pretending we do. I wish we would stop throwing away the beauty that is right in front of us today, devaluing what is, in order to make heaven look that much better in contrast.

I believe that God and heaven and all their beauty are closer to this moment than they will ever be again.

We picture heaven as the farthest-off thing. It is "after" - after we die, after Jesus comes back, after, after, after. Could it be that pushing heaven off into eternity is our way of avoiding its actual existence? That might be useful if the uncertainty we feel about heaven makes us uncomfortable.

It might also be a great way to avoid a potential responsibility we have, to *help* heaven somehow.

Maybe we are more comfortable keeping heaven at a distance. Maybe we are more comfortable showing up to a church and being told *about* God and *about* heaven. Like being told what skydiving is like. It's safer. It's faster too. And infinitely duller.

August 2, 2016

What is this time for? What am I supposed to be doing? I feel so little direction. What's my goal? What are my dreams? What are my responsibilities? Where does rest fit in? Grief?

If I'm crippled, then trying to be "productive" is a mistake. Healing is more productive than the type of "productive" I feel drawn to - the type which reminds people I still exist.

I'm afraid if I sit still to rest, to heal, to grieve… I'll disappear. People will forget me. I'll lose my chance to make my mark on the world.

Sad and Consistent

Tonight I realized that this entire day I was anxious and extremely sad.

I had no idea. It just felt like a "regular" day. I did my work and mowed the lawn. But the whole time I felt so anxious. Playing songs and conversations and scenarios inside my head, mostly subconscious. Non-stop. Like a constant noise inside.

I had to lay down after dinner. I thought I was sick. Then it hit me that I was extremely sad and missed Olivia. As soon as I allowed myself to feel that and to cry, I felt physically fine. I got up and played the rest of the night with my other daughter. I felt sad the entire time - very sad - but I also felt like a whole person; I felt alive.

I would rather feel sad and consistent all the way through than to appear fine and be at war with myself.

Come Back

Come back to the dish you're washing.

Come back to the lawn you're mowing.

Come back to the kid you're playing with.

Come back to the song you're singing.

Come back to the meal you're eating.

Come back to the teeth you're brushing.

Come back to the breath you're breathing.

Come back to here.

Come back to now.

Come back to where you are.

August 10, 2016

I'm going insane.

Ruth has felt sick the last two nights, and for some reason, that is killing me with fear and worry. I know it's not logical. It's just… "things are not okay." Then Charlie complained that he felt tired and had a hard time breathing. Again, it's not okay. All I can think about is that my kids are not okay.

I feel panic.

I know it's not a big deal. Ruth puked a couple weeks ago. It was fine. Charlie did too. Also fine. 24 hours later it's like it never happened. All the kids were happy and playing today. They're fine.

But I feel panic. "They're not okay."

I can't be anywhere except trying to help them in my head. If they're not okay, I'm not okay. That seems important. And unhealthy. If the kids aren't okay, I can still be okay. Otherwise, I'm not much help to them anyway.

Still, it's how I feel. How do I become free of these feelings, of this anxiety about sickness?

It was the same when Olivia was alive. I feel the same now as I did then.

I'm afraid of losing my ability to take care of my family.

I don't want to be weak. Useless. Powerless. If my kids are sick, I can't help them. If I'm sick, I can't help them.

Helpless. That's how I felt with Olivia.

I feel helpless. I am helpless. Olivia died. She died while I was out. Far out of my control.

But…

In this moment, everything is okay. I'm okay. My family is okay. Olivia is okay.

The Strength
To Let Go

The strength and courage to let go.

To let go of the future.

To let go of the past.

To let go of everything that is not, and to return to what is.

To come back to where we are.

This is so much more powerful than any amount of control we could ever have.

August 23, 2016

I lost my daughter too.

I went through the same trauma. I also carried Heather. I put all the things she couldn't do on my shoulders. I took care of our family. Why am I expected now to be perfect, and she's allowed to blow up whenever she's upset?

What do I do now? Probably just wait. I want to hit her - to take the respect she won't give me.

What do I do with my hate?

Probably "let it go".

I'd rather hurt someone.

If she would just apologize…

I hate this.

The Battle

Yesterday morning I finished yoga and was supposed to "get up from my laying position and feel good about using these 30 minutes to improve my breathing and strength." I stayed down.

My body would not move except for a bunch of tears streaming onto the floor. This position feels more honest to me right now than any upright, contributing-to-society position. Right now, I would rather be honest than great. I would rather be cohesive than impressive.

A pile of parts on the floor. I have had this picture in my head, and yesterday my body was able to meet down there with my mind and my heart. It was awful. But it was not hell. Hell isn't that beautiful.

A couple of weeks ago I had to lay down. I thought I was sick until I realized I was just sad. I allowed myself to cry, then got up and felt fine. It was painful. But it was not hell.

Hell isn't that honest.

I don't really care about the afterlife hell right now. I'm trying to live today; what happens after death feels too impractical. But I am becoming increasingly aware of another, more immediate and available hell. One I feel much more drawn to than the afterlife one. One I feel much more familiar with.

I have spent a lot of time here. Separated. Fragmented. Part of me is still back in real life, in moments which actually are. But my mind is here, in the future, controlling: deciding what others think, deciding what things will happen to me and to my family, deciding how and why, creating my own universe. Part of me is here; the rest of me is back in real life. And in being both places, I basically am being nowhere. I'm not being at all. I'm worrying. I'm controlling. But it's pretending. None of it is real, and while I stay neither here nor there—while I remain in a state of non-being, of non-living—real life continues, and *I miss it.*

Non-being. Separated not only from my Self, but from my wife, my kids, my family and friends, and if God is life and God is real, then also separated from God. In a prison of worry, anxiety, and the responsibility to carry the world on my own shoulders. Isolation. Hell.

Hell is where life is not, like darkness is where light is not. Life is only here, only in this moment. Hell is everywhere else.

I will admit right now that I may be completely theologically wrong. That's fine. I have no interest in being right. I do have great interest in shining light on something when I see it. Here is what I see:

I see life being skipped over by people who always believe they should be somewhere other than where they are. I see Industry helping people *go* - anywhere else, right now. I see a culture sitting on the starting line of their journey, never taking the first step because Fear has them shopping for better shoes before they will start. I see this in our culture. In our work. In our churches. Everywhere. I see this in myself the most.

I also see people waking up, lots of them.

I see heaven coming. Not on the horizon or in the afterlife. I see it coming from right here - from within me, from within people. People are waking up and realizing that heaven is in our possession - a gift given to us with a charge: to usher it in.

We are the delivery system.

I don't think "ushering heaven in" looks like believing or doing the right things. I think it probably looks more like stopping: stopping to talk with our kids about legos (literally, as I was typing that my son came in and asked me to fix his lego guy), stopping to just be still for a while, stopping to pay attention to our breath. Stopping and allowing ourselves to cry about something, or to laugh. Stopping the universe-creating, the future-living, the researching all uncertainty and discomfort out from our lives...

I am sure it starts with stopping. Quiet. Rest.

I don't know exactly what it looks like for you, but I believe each of us deep down knows *exactly* what it looks like for ourself. I know it will start with a lot of letting go. And a lot more trust than we are comfortable with. And a lot more uncertainty, discomfort, and even pain than we would like. But deep down it is what we all want: Real Life.

We want to *live*. We want to *be*. No longer fragmented, no longer separated from where we really are, no longer isolated from each other, from God, and from ourselves.

If we want this—if we really want to live—we are going to have to fight.

The battle between hell and heaven is for the moments happening right now. Neither hell nor heaven cares about our silly future.

The battle is real and it is now. And you know exactly what you need to do.

A New Enemy

I'm sure there is a book somewhere that says Month Five is worse than Month One, and I'm sure reading it wouldn't make any difference.

This week I have turned into a hateful angry person. I have blown up at home multiple times. Everything Heather says hits me wrong. I'm embarrassed that my kids have seen me this way. Not to mention Heather, and probably some neighbors.

I feel myself becoming someone I don't respect. It feels like there is nothing I can do about it, just like I can't do anything about the weather. Or Olivia. It's all just sort-of taking its course. I have such an extremely uncomfortable sense of no-control.

For the past couple of years, I have been waving the flag of "Fear is the enemy" and I have been fighting Fear on a daily basis. I think I have done pretty well at it. But I feel like the battle has shifted for me, and it shifted without me noticing.

Control is my new enemy, or the desire for it.

I just want to feel like I have a handle on something. Anything. I want to feel like something is under control.

I have been drawn to researching better tools more than usual lately, and I think this explains why. It is something for me to control. With better tools, I have the perception of controlling my work and my life that much better.

I have felt the need for our house to be clean, even more than usual. It's something controllable which makes me feel incrementally better.

I have been more on top of practice and exercise than ever—something I can control.

But despite the amount of care I put into these things, they are relatively unimportant things to me—much less important to me than things like Olivia's life, our other kids' health, my health, my career, Heather's words... the things most important to me... the things I have absolutely no control over.

So I grab onto the things I can control. But it is not helping.

Deep down I know I didn't have what it took. I couldn't save Olivia. I can't protect my kids from everything. I can't make Heather respect me. The reality is, I am not in control.

I hate the feeling. But I think I am making the battle about the wrong thing. The *exact* wrong thing. I can't be concerned with regaining a sense of control. I must be willing to accept the reality of my situation, and the situation is and has always been: I am not in control.

I am not in control.

Freedom is on the other side of this truth. The most important things to us are outside of our control. Maybe that is why they are so valuable to us - we know they are only ours because they have been given.

Is the battle shifting, or am I just experiencing a new facet of the same fight?

Fear is becoming less of the issue. It is there. It is not helping anything, but I can't get rid of it either. I can't just "not be afraid". I can only pretend... But what if I can be okay with that? What if I can allow Fear to be there - to give it that freedom without my normal response?

My normal response to Fear is control. What if instead, I choose to respond by letting go? Wouldn't that take away all of Fear's power?

September 1, 2016

Today Heather said she didn't want to move forward with me. She said she can't stand me.

There's nothing I can do. That's it.

Fine. I don't need her to like me, agree with me, support me, respect me. I still have responsibilities. I still have to heal.

I am alone.

Continuing Life With Olivia

Today is six months since Olivia died.

It is still so hard to comprehend, staring at this grave, that my daughter's body is just a few feet beneath the new grass now growing. Waves of sadness still hit me like a wall when I see a picture of her. I still feel an irresistible urge to touch my phone screen when a photo of her pops up. I still feel the dull ache of loss, the emptiness she left, and it physically hurts. It destroys our bodies. We are walking through these days with feet made of cement. It is just really hard. Much harder than anyone could have prepared us for.

But I would not trade this time.

This pain and suffering connects us to Olivia.

In the same way that avoiding the pain during her life

would have meant missing her life, I think avoiding the pain now means missing the possibility of *continuing life with Olivia*.

That is a possibility I didn't know existed six months ago: continuing life *with* Olivia. Not the memory of her—memories fade. Not the idea of her—ideas distort over time. But actually continuing life *with* her, actually *her*.

My biggest fear six months ago was that Olivia would fade over time - a dream we had once. Six months in, I feel like *I* have faded. I feel like everything I knew before has faded. Olivia's smell has completely faded from her clothes. My memories of her have faded. But *her*, Olivia the person, Olivia our daughter... she has not faded.

She can't fade because we are still here.

We are completely different people, changed by our time with her.

The only way for Olivia to fade is for us to resume life as the people we used to be—something we can only do by pretending.

It is tempting to pretend. The "new us" is damaged goods, broken pieces of people from the past, in a pile on the floor. But we are real. And we are beautiful, even if we are not functional. And that is very much a manifestation of Olivia the person.

Not her memory, but her. She can't fade. She is right here, in my hands as I write these words.

Continuing life with Olivia. It isn't possible apart from the pain and suffering we are experiencing. So we accept the pain and suffering as a gift.

We would not trade this.

September 22, 2016

Directionless. Well, not direction*less*, but confused about direction.

It feels like I can be doing a lot of different things, from self-care to writing to song-writing to concerts to projects, albums, videos… lots I can do.

Also, a constant pull to do nothing, to just be.

I keep coming back to "Do the next thing." Not the next project or next move. Just literally the very next thing. Like, I want to go do yoga next. Actually, use the bathroom first. Then yoga. Then probably voice practice. But even that far is too far to plan.

Next is usually clear for me. Everything else is dark. I guess that's all the direction I need.

September 25, 2016

I'm trying to do what I said I'd do: remain in the position we learned to hold while we held Olivia.

It's difficult to rest in the midst of disaster.

To rest in the wake of it feels impossible.

What do I know?

- It's OK to feel this way.
- It will be OK.

The Process

Things take a lot longer to process and to feel than we give ourselves time for.

We're still experiencing that first night in the hospital with Olivia, when they handed me my baby who I thought was dead. I didn't process that then. I was just surviving. I'm processing it now.

Culture-wise, I feel alien about this. I feel like I must be pretty messed up to be so slow at processing what seems to take others only weeks or days.

The truth is, no one can process as fast as we have learned we should. Instead, we have learned to ignore, to stuff it down, to cover it up, skip over, and to quickly move to the next item.

Process is not a luxury we allow ourselves.

But life is a process!

October 17, 2016

I'm out. I'm done.

I have no money. We're in debt. I've failed. I can barely keep from hurting myself. I want to scream. To break something. I want to die. I can't make anything happen. I'm a loser. An amateur. A failure. I'm on the verge of tears. And insanity. I can't take any more steps. I'm finished. What do I do?

Somehow I was fine during Olivia's life. But now I'm not. Why?! Why is it worse now than it was before?! I just want a break. I want to feel like things are okay. I'm so tired. So lonely.

What will Christmas be like? I'm such a failure.

What do I do?

Let go. Trust. Rest. Be. I'm doing great things with you. I am with you. It's not your job to be

with me. Or to provide. Or to impact. Only to trust, and to obey.

But, what do I do?

Commit, fully.

To what?

Your path.

I commit.

Then, rest.

Move On

Since Olivia died, I've felt rushed to move on.

"Moving on" brings a picture to my mind of crying all my tears, then standing up and getting back to it. Like a pit-stop, it was necessary, but now I'm good and ready to go.

I fantasize about walking back into the figurative room of life, all my friends seeing me. I strongly announce, "I'm back." "He's back!" Everyone cheers.

It feels nice, but I already know that it will never happen. I will never say those words. Not because I will never heal, but because the Me who was is gone. He will never be back. And I'm not going to pretend.

But a new Me is emerging.

Part of me is buried a mile from my house with my daughter, a rubber giraffe, a pumpkin rattle held together by a piece of scotch tape, and a dress my wife knit two years ago. Not just a part of me—the best part of me I had to offer.

Part of Olivia is buried in us. Everything we see, every song we hear, everything I write, every conversation we have—everything is affected by Olivia and somehow experienced with her. It's not just her memory. It's more than that. It's *her*. Part of her is in us. Not just a part of her—the best part of her she had to offer.

I would never take that part of me out of her casket. I would never take that part of her out of me. Not in a million years.

But it is a new reality, and I don't know how to be this new person. Nothing feels familiar. Nothing is comfortable. I feel like an alien. All I can do is accept the change and trust the process.

A new Me is emerging. This is beauty from ashes. It's life. Our life. We can't "move on" from that. We wouldn't if we could.

So if we are not moving on, what is ahead for us?

In front of us is uncertain - a dark room. Also, in front of us is Life. It's both. It's always that way.

Life is a dark room. We have to accept the uncertainty and the clumsiness of it, and walk into the darkness anyway.

Life is a dark room. But darkness doesn't scare us the way

it used to.

What is ahead for us? Uncertainty. A dark room. *Life*.

Life is ahead.

November 16, 2016

I'm full-on panicking again. I can't control the worry.

It's been three days straight. I can't take a full breath.
I'm absent-minded. Paranoid. I'm guessing everyone
I know is judging me for not being more productive.

My body is tired. It feels like someone is constantly
choking me. My body feels balled up. Crunched.
Clenched. Crushed.

I want to buy things I don't need. I feel obsessed.

The band's credit payment is due today. I don't have it.
I don't even know what I can do about it.

I feel so alone.

I can't see past my cloud of self-hatred and self-disgust.
I feel like I'll never be free. I'm in a vice. I know I'm the
one causing it, but I can't seem to let go.

December 12, 2016

I am out of sorts. I can't produce anything. I want to make art, but I'm still so tired. I feel lost. Out of gas. Broken down.

Patience.

Trust.

Rest.

That feels impossible.

Frozen

Today I was looking back at my New Year journal entries. It is striking how much my outlook on life has changed in just a few years.

In 2014, I had two pages of goals with daily, weekly, and monthly routines and checkpoints to help me reach those goals.

In 2015, my goal was to fully experience Olivia's birth, which was supposed to be the only few minutes we would have with her. I had a bunch of plans—a "train schedule" I called it—for how we would recover and then continue growing Hello Industry (our band) starting that February. I gave myself one month to grieve.

In 2016, Olivia had been alive almost a year. She defied all odds and had convinced us she was here to stay. Her birthday was coming. I wrote in my journal that my only goal for the year was to live each moment, fully. Nothing else.

How beautiful and how powerful that one little girl, who can not even hold her head up, who is so severely disabled that she doesn't even know she's disabled, can transform the mind and heart of a 35-year-old man—a stubborn, overly driven, overly self-aware, fearful man. Powerful, powerful little Olivia.

This year, I can't even make a goal. I can't bear to look forward. I am too overwhelmed to look back.

I am frozen.

Here is what I need to hear today:

You are frozen, but you are in the River's Current, and the Current is moving. The Current is not stuck. And at least you are here. Most of your life you have been everywhere but where you are. Maybe here is not comfortable or clear. Maybe here is not "successful" or famous. But here is where you are.

This is life, and you are finally living it.

This year I can't even make a goal. So instead I will borrow last year's one:

Live fully the life that is in front of me. Be present with my family. Make meaningful art. Refuse to worry.

Honestly, that seems impossible to me right now. I feel like I was a better man one year ago. But I will try. Or maybe better, I will let it happen. I will trust the Current.

I am frozen, but the Current is not.

January 7, 2017

Happy birthday (two years) Olivia. We love you. We would happily do it all again, and again, and again. You are and forever will be our 4th child. Our 2nd daughter. Our fun-loving, beautiful, talented, determined, perfect little girl.

This Is Life

Yesterday we sang happy birthday at Olivia's grave, sent off a floating lantern (which the boys and I went running after in a panic when it burst into flames and came floating down out of the sky a half-mile away in our neighborhood), and we had a cake and shared our favorite memories of Olivia. Heather and I watched videos of her after the kids went to sleep.

Yesterday was not an easy day, but there was also nothing wrong with it. It was right and good. Hard and sad. Also happy. It was perfect. The same is true of the past two years. Not only would we do it again, but we would not change any of it if we could—even, and especially, the hard parts.

This is life and we embrace it.

REST is the pathway
to the present.
The present is the doorway
to LIFE.
Without REST, there is
no LIVING.

January 12, 2016

After showering and exercise, I feel like I'm already done for the day. I haven't even gotten to voice work, practice, writing, etc.

I feel foggy and lost.

Tired.

Guilty.

I know to let those feelings happen. To not try to change them. Let the waves come and let them go. But it feels like I'm falling apart.

When will I feel drive again? Is drive even a good thing?

I don't know.

February 3, 2016

The tendency, the habit, to fill the space.

I need that space to remain empty.

Especially now.

We're grieving. Mourning. Healing.

That requires space.

But I feel like I'm wasting time, or being lazy, or failing.

So I fill the space with doing. Good things or bad things - they all fill the space.

But what I'm adding isn't adding at all. It's consuming the space. It's consuming me.

I'm programmed to "fix it." To make it happen. To figure it out. To control.

I'm being reprogrammed. I'm being healed.

Be, before doing.

Let the space remain.

February 7, 2017

Man. Another horrible day. I screamed obscenities out of nowhere multiple times today. Everything felt broken. My relationship with Heather. The van. The band's money. The dishwasher. My voice. Everything. Me.

I feel hopeless. Stuck. Trapped. Incompetent.

What's really frustrating is that when I feel good, I can do things, make art, get along with Heather, be okay…

I feel fine, and then I am fine.

I feel horrible, and then I am horrible.

I'm a slave to my feelings.

This is why people use drugs.

February 8, 2017

We just got in the biggest fight so far. I punched a wall. My hand hurts too much to write...

February 13, 2017

My hand still hurts. What a hard couple of weeks. Pukes from all the kids. Fevers. Double-flu. Heather was sick in bed for almost a week. HUGE fights with Heather. The worst fight ever.

Everyone is better now, almost. So I'm "back to it." I guess. Except with less energy and even less optimism or motivation.

I'm angry at God.

I'm sick of doing the right thing or trying to. It doesn't help anything. I feel like I've given everything, and the needle has barely moved.

So what? What now??

It's not a marathon. You don't have to be strong. It's okay to fall apart. You can only be where you are. You don't have to control. The waves will come and they will go.

Keep going.

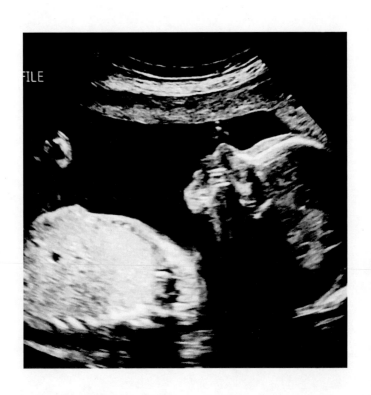

I may write another song
Maybe even the perfect one
But it won't ever be the same
I may take another try
To pick my feet up for another mile
But it won't ever be the same

I don't want to dance again.
Tell the music not to play.
I can see her, I can feel her face
I don't want to dance again.

Seasons change & memories fade
Tears dry but scars remain.
Things are never gonna be the same...

May 2, 2016

One minute I'm frozen. The next I'm hopeful. The next I'm sad. Then furious. Then I record a couple tracks. Then I'm too embarrassed to raise my head.

Be here while you're here. Be there while you're there.

I recorded three takes of "Dance Again" today. I compared it with a previous take - the old take sounds sonically superior. Better timing and pitch too. But it sounds like… a recitation. Robotic. Notes and words.

Today's recording isn't as perfect, but it feels like a real moment in time. That's important. Isn't that all I can hope for?

[This take ended up being the final recording of Dance Again.]

The Door

There is a door in front of me today.

The door is there every moment because the door *is* the moment. Through this door, within each moment, is life. Life is nowhere else - only here, only now, in this moment. That is the nature of life - it happens when and where it is, and then it is gone.

I am afraid of this door - for lots of reasons, most of which I can't even articulate. So I rarely walk through it. I actively avoid it. But it is always there in front of me, open and waiting.

The door looks like all kinds of things: My wife. My kids. Time alone. A book. A meal. My work. Every time, God is there. It is where God lives. Also every time, I am there— the true Me, the real Me. Whatever is real is there.

Everything outside this door is artificial. It is fantasy. My fantasy. Some of this fantasy is wonderful. Most of it is horrible. Worst case scenarios and people's worst possible impressions of me are here, outside the door, outside of the moment, outside of reality.

Why do I work so hard to stay outside this door when everything I want is inside, and my worst nightmares are outside? I don't know. I think it has to do with fear. I have a feeling it has even more to do with control.

May 14, 2017

Come back to where you are.

Don't run away from or cut off the pain.

Let it remain. Be with it.

Be where you are.

May 14, 2017

As soon as I get more than one step ahead, things leave the present - I lose my balance. I'm no longer centered.

Haven't I been hearing this for a long time now? "Come back to where you are. Only in this moment. Only do the next thing." Any attention spread beyond that is taking me away from where I am.

But it's so hard! There are bills. Debt. Reputation. Numbers which show how bad I'm failing. What about those??

Those are not real. They're just thoughts and perceptions. What is real is what is here and now.

Trust. Rest. Quiet.

Interesting.

When I trust, I become excited to work. Work feels

like play.

When I trust, I think much bigger. Things seem possible.

When I trust, I can breathe and rest while I'm not working... and when I am working.

When I trust, I become available to others, because my problems are already being taken care of. *I am being taken care of.*

Ben Is Here!

Nothing has felt as expected.

I expected to feel terrified all the way through. I *was* terrified, until he was born. I think then it was real, so it was fine. Or, *I* was fine.

There were some complications, but it was fine when they happened. I mean, *it* was not fine—it was very scary—but *I* was fine.

I'm very confused now. I had expected to be devastated.

I'm not.

I feel happy. Ben is here and he is so cute! So sweet. And doing so well.

I'm so confused.

I don't want to forget Olivia.

Also, I don't want to miss Ben.

I choose to be *here*, wherever "here" is, in these moments.

These confusing moments.

These terrifying moments.

These exciting moments.

These dark moments.

These happy moments.

These perfect moments.

These beautiful moments.

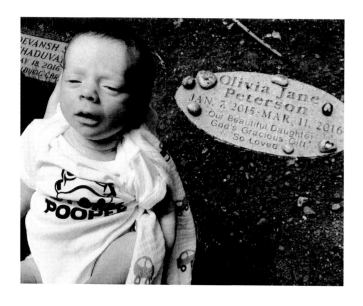

Special thanks to Jim Phillips. Thank you for walking with us through all of it. Thank you for the many reminders about who we are: we are the planters and waterers. We will continue to practice what you taught us. We will try. Please kiss Olivia for us.

Nathan Peterson is a singer/songwriter from Illinois. He and his wife Heather are the parents of five children: Jude, Charlie, Ruth, Olivia, and Benjamin.

Nathan's previous book, <u>So Am I: 14 Months of Life, Living, and Letting Go</u>, is available on Amazon and direct at the address below.

Both <u>So Am I</u> and <u>Dance Again</u> were written with matching music albums. The albums are available on iTunes/Spotify/Amazon and direct at the address below.

More about Nathan and his work here:
http://nathanpeterson.net

Made in United States
North Haven, CT
02 November 2021

10792275R00067